Sometimes a few toys were shared by all the children in the family. Many toys were home made.

The three toys on the right are made of tin. They were called "penny toys" as they could be bought from street sellers for one penny ($\frac{1}{2}$p).

Children's toys in 1900 included draughts, ludo, skittles, wooden building blocks or toy soldiers. Some children were lucky enough to be given one of the first Meccano sets.

"I had a doll which was wax-faced. When it was my turn for a bath I put the doll down in front of the fire. When I got out – poor thing – her face was all gone!"

On Sundays all toys and games were put away.

Things to do

Start to make a book about *Entertainment in 1900*.
Write about how children 80 years ago entertained themselves.
Draw some of the toys and games they played with at home.

Find out what a diabolo is and how you play with it.

Ask someone older than 70 what they called their dolls.

Family entertainment

This family has got together for a family celebration. When they have eaten their tea they will entertain each other. Families read and played games like blind man's buff, forfeits and charades. "Happy Families" and "Beat Your Neighbour" were popular family card games.

**"We loved charades.
We were great ones for dressing up
and playing charades."**

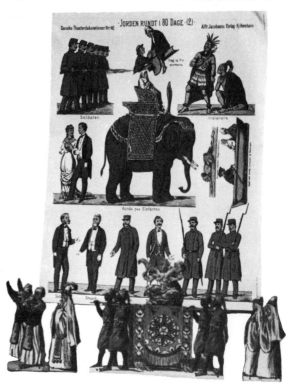

Toy theatres were popular, too. Children stuck sheets of characters and scenery on to cardboard, and cut them out. You can see some of the characters in this photograph.

Families and friends watched plays acted on a model stage.

4

"My family was fond of music and singing. We used to play on the piano and sing as a family group."

This picture shows an elderly couple by their piano. Notice the music on the piano. They sang popular songs in 1900 such as:

"Come into the garden, Maud"

"Honeysuckle and the bee"

"Grandfather's clock"

Musical boxes and gramophones were popular. The gramophone worked by winding up a clockwork motor. A needle took the sound from a wax cylinder and sent it out through a tin trumpet.

Things to do

Write about and draw a picture of family entertainment in 1900.

Ask someone older than 70 how their family entertained. Find out what songs they sang. Perhaps you could record elderly people singing popular songs of 1900.

You can buy Pollock's toy theatres in some shops. Or you can make one of your own using an old box for the theatre.

"The pictures"

**"They used to have a
magic lantern session. 'Twinkle,
twinkle, little star' or something.
They'd show us a
few pictures of different lands."**

Magic lantern shows were a popular
form of entertainment in 1900.
They were shown either at home
or at local halls.

Oil-burning magic lantern

There were toys for children which showed moving pictures.
These included kaleidoscopes, flicker books and shadow puppets.

This is a zoetrope. You look through the slots
in the side of the drum. When the drum is
spinning round, the pictures appear to be
moving. The movement is jerky, like
cartoon films.

Zoetrope strips

"It was the beginning of the pictures. Flickering pictures shown in an old hall. You sat on long wooden benches. I used to go there for sixpence ($2\frac{1}{2}$p)."

Look at this photograph of people watching a black and white film at "the pictures".
Look for:

—the screen on which the film is being shown. These early films
   were jerky and often covered in spots. They only lasted a few minutes.
—the piano player who is playing music to go with the silent film.
Sometimes moving picture films were shown as part of a music hall show.

There were toy picture projectors 80 years ago. Children could buy
film strips of sports, horse racing, dancing and other activities.

Thing to do

Ask someone elderly if they had any "picture" toys
when they were your age. Some people made their own.
Perhaps they can show you how to make one.

Make your own zoetrope. Use card to make the drum.
Colour the picture strips.

7

Outdoor games

"Children played in the streets much more than they do now."

In 1900 children spent hours playing in the street. There was not as much traffic about as today. Many outdoor games were made up using buttons, cigarette cards and skipping ropes. Skipping games were very popular. Children often made up words to sing as they skipped.

Hoops were a favourite toy 80 years ago. The girl in the picture is skipping with her hoop. Some hoops were made of iron and some were made of wood. Hoops were called "bowles" in Wales, and "girths" in Durham.

Bedford 1902

"We used to play marbles. But mother didn't like the girls getting on the floor. She said, 'You're dirtying your clothes up. You're not to do that.'"

Roller skating was a popular craze. The skates cost about 5s 6d (27½p) a pair.

Advertisement from "Black and White" magazine 1900

8

This is a spell. It was used in the game of knur and spell. The knur was a small ball which was placed in the cup on the spell.

The player hit the right-hand end bar of the spell with a club. This sent the knur into the air. The knur was then hit with the club as far as possible.

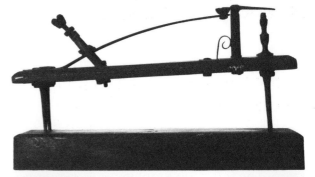

This picture shows a knur and spell game in progress.
Look for:
—the knur and spell at the bottom left
—the clubs held by the man and the boy
—the crowd.

A simpler version of this game was known as "tip-cat". Other popular street games and toys were hopscotch, fivestones or chuckstones, and whipping tops.

Things to do

Try to find out what outdoor games were played 80 years ago in the area where you live.

Write down the words to skipping songs.
In your book make two lists. Call one list *Games then.*
Write about games in 1900. Call the other list *Games now.*
Write about the games you play.

Sports and hobbies

"We kicked a rag ball around. We couldn't afford to buy a leather one so we used to make one of rags tied together."

Football was the most popular sport 80 years ago. The F.A. Cup Final in 1901 between Tottenham Hotspur and Sheffield United was watched by 110,000 people.

Chesterton Victoria football team, Cambridge 1905–6

Cricket was played on village greens around the country and by children in the streets. Tennis, rugby, boxing, fishing and horse racing were also popular sports.

"When the river froze over we went skating. But you had to be careful."

River Ouse, Bedford 1891

Cycling became a popular hobby for those who could afford a bicycle. Not many children's bicycles were made.

Despite their long skirts, women rode bicycles. Cycling Clubs were formed.

Cambridge Ladies Junior Cycling Club 1898

Many children made collections of butterflies, pressed wild flowers, shells or stamps. A favourite hobby was keeping scrapbooks of newspaper cuttings.

Things to do

Look again at the pictures of sports. Notice the clothes.
Now draw or paint a picture of a sport 80 years ago.

Ask someone old you know what hobbies they had when they were your age. Did they play any sports? Did they go to watch any matches? Did they make a scrapbook or keep an album? Did they collect anything? What happened to their collection?

Local customs

Bampton morris dancers, Oxfordshire 1900

The picture above shows morris dancers.
Look for:

—the 6 dancers waving handkerchiefs
—the musician playing a violin, on the right
—the people watching the dancing.

May Day, Kempston, Bedfords

"We sang and danced. People came from miles around."

Many children watched
or took part in plays,
singing or dancing
on special days during
the year. Each village
or town had its own way
of celebrating.

Mummers, Northill, Bedfordshire

These boys are about
to act a play. It was
a local custom in East
Anglia to do this each
year on Plough Monday.
Look for:

—the boy dressed as a woman
—two boys with their faces blacked
—the decorated hats
—the sashes worn by four boys.

Things to do

Find out about local customs in the area where you live.

Write about taking part in a local play or dance 80 years ago.
Paint a picture of people taking part in a local custom.

Ask someone elderly what they remember about local customs
when they were your age.

Street entertainers

Dumfries, Scotland 1902

**"It was our only chance of seeing a bear.
He was a lovely creature to look at, but rather alarming."**

In the picture of the dancing bear
look for:
—the large bear standing on its
   hind legs
—the muzzle over the bear's mouth
—the heavy pole held by the man
—the bare feet of some of the children
—the boy on the right pointing at
   the camera.

This street musician has
a gramophone on his cart.

London 1909

14

"We used to have quite a number of these entertainers come round."

Children who lived in towns in 1900 saw many street entertainers.
There were:

bands
buskers (musicians)
organ grinders
jugglers
dancing dogs
Punch and Judy shows

This family toured round London doing acrobatic displays.

London street artistes 1890

Aunt Sally was a popular attraction at village fetes. Sticks were thrown at clay pipes stuck in the head.

Things to do

In your book, write *Street entertainers*. Describe the entertainers who came down the street in 1900. Pretend you were there watching them.

Draw a picture of children watching street entertainment.

15

Fairs and circuses

Pat Collins' motors, Nottingham Goose Fair 1908

"Fairs used to come on all the major holidays."

Fairs were a great favourite with children and adults alike.
There were swings and roundabouts, hoop-la stalls and coconut shies.
The picture above shows children and adults watching people on one of the rides. Notice the steam engine on the right. This drove the roundabout.

There were also many sideshow booths. You could pay to go in and watch boxing and wrestling matches, acrobats, magicians and strange attractions like "the bearded lady".

This picture shows a portable theatre. Look for:

Studt's portable theatre 1908

—the girl acrobats
—the decorations on the booth
—the cost of admission
—the time of the next performance
—the notice showing that pictures will be shown. This was a new attraction at fairs 80 years ago.

"I loved walking through the town with the circus."

Ginett's circus arriving at Chichester

Small tented circuses travelled round the country. They had clowns, acrobats and animals. This picture shows a circus arriving at a new town. They paraded through the streets to the showground.

Things to do

Ask someone elderly what they remember about fairs and circuses.

Pretend either that you run a sideshow *or* that you are a performer in a circus in 1900. Write about what you do. Draw a picture to go with your story.

The theatre and concerts

Prince's Theatre, Bristol 1899–1900

"I only went to one pantomime. I was taken to 'Robinson Crusoe'. It was nothing like the story in the book."

Children in 1900 were taken to the theatre to see pantomimes. They were put on at Christmas and Easter. Look at the picture above of "Aladdin". The pantomimes had brilliant scenery and costumes.

Poster for Mr. Albert Chevalier's recitals 1905

TOWN HALL, Oxford.
Plan & Tickets at
Messrs. A. SCOTT HARRIS & Co., Music Warehouse, 124, High Street.
Doors open 7.30. Commence at 8 Carriage at 10

Thurs. & Fri., Oct. 19th & 20th, at 8.
- - TWO NIGHTS ONLY - -
Prices, 4/-, 3/-, 2/-, 1/-.
Unreserved Ticket Holders admitted by Early Door at 7.15 without extra charge

MR . . .
ALBERT CHEVALIER'S RECITALS
From the Queen's Hall and St. James's Hall, London.

MR. CHEVALIER'S PRO-GRAMME will be selected from the following:
"Hammer."
"Hif not, why not ?"
"The Village Constable."
"Wot fur do 'es luv ai?"
"The Veteran."
"Mafekin' Night."
"An Old Bachelor."
"A Fallen Star."
"The Poet."
"M. Armand Thibault."
"My Country Cousin."
"The Curate."
"The Workhouse Man."
"The Coster's Serenade."
"Our Court Ball."
"Our Little Nipper."

Re-appearance after his remarkably successful second American Tour,
SUPPORTED BY
Miss FLOSSIE BEHRENS (Whistling Soloist)   Miss TRESSILIAN DAVY (Soprano),
Mr. ISIDORE MARCIL, Basso, and Mr. ALFRED H. WEST (Solo Pianist and Accompanist).
Manager, Mr. CHARLES INGLE.

18

Poster for the Hippodrome, Tonypandy, Wales 1909

Sometimes children went to local halls to watch mixed programmes of entertainment.

Look at this poster. Read it carefully. Notice the variety of things to see. Look for:

—Will Stone's electric bioscope. This was a film projector. The projectors used before 1900 often caught fire.
—"On the Banks of the Ganges" which was a magic lantern display of pictures taken in India
—the playlet presented by the Forestiers
—the admission prices.

Things to do

Ask someone elderly to tell you if there was a theatre near where they lived. Did they ever go?

Find out about the music hall songs, the musical comedies and melodrama. Try to collect old song music or theatre programmes.

Write about a concert at a local town hall in 1900. Look again at the poster.

Seaside entertainment

**"The seaside was a way of having a playground
with an enormous variety of activities."**

"We fished and played on the sand. We had boat trips."

By 1900 more families could afford a holiday. In Lancashire, for example, the mills closed in the summer for a "wakes week".

There was plenty of entertainment
at the seaside. Here is a picture of
a Punch and Judy show on the beach.

*Punch and Judy,
Ilfracombe 1890s*

There were donkey rides,
firework displays, boxing
contests and circuses
at the seaside resorts.
You could go down
the pier and see concerts
and peepshows.

"There was a brass band on the front."

Here you can see Uncle Mack's minstrels show.
Look for:
—the minstrels wearing black and white make-up
—the clothes worn by the people in the audience
—the bathing machines on wheels. These were pulled down
   to the sea. People changed into their bathing suits in them.

*Broadstairs
1908*

Things to do

In your book, write *Seaside entertainment*.
Describe a day at the seaside in 1900. Draw or paint a picture of seaside entertainment.

Picture postcards were first sent by holidaymakers at the seaside
80 years ago. They often had funny cartoons on them. See if you can
collect old picture postcards.

Days out

This picture shows a small zoo at the seaside.

"Oh you used to stand fascinated. It was wonderful. We thought we'd seen all there was."

Yarmouth, August Bank Holiday 1891

Many families could only afford to go to the seaside for the day. There were special trains at weekends and Bank Holidays.

Regent's Park Zoo, London 1902

Day trips to zoos were very popular. Children rode on elephants and camels.

"You had to go up a ladder to get on the animal's back."

Look at this picture of children riding on a dromedary (an Arabian camel with one hump).

The only holidays some children had
were Sunday School outings.
Some lucky children from towns went
to holiday farms on school trips.

This is a paddle steamboat.
It took people for boat trips
on the River Thames in London.

Some children in 1900 were taken to
waxworks and to large exhibitions.

'Thomas More' 1907

Things to do

Ask someone older than 70 about going on day trips.
Where did they go? What did they see?
Who did they go with? How did they get there?
Write down what they tell you in your book.

Collect pictures about days out in 1900.

Pub entertainment

This picture shows men
in the back yard
of a public house.
They are playing cards
and drinking and smoking.

Inside the pub they played
games like skittles,
shove ha'penny, dominoes
and "ringing the bull".
Find out about these
games.

They were sometimes entertained by musicians playing
piano, accordion, violin, mouth organ or tin whistle.

The following museums have displays of things
and events mentioned in this book:

Museum of Childhood, Bethnal Green, London
Museum of Childhood, High Street, Edinburgh
Museum of Childhood, Menai Bridge,
    Gwynedd, Wales
Castle Museum, Tower Street, York
The Museum of London, London Wall, London
The Precinct Toy Collection, Harnet Street,
    Sandwich, Kent
Doll Museum, Oken's House, Castle Street,
    Warwick

The Norton Collection, Davenal House,
    Bromsgrove, Hereford & Worcester
North of England Open Air Museum, Beamish,
    Stanley, County Durham
Cambridge and County Folk Museum, Castle
    Street, Cambridge
Thursford Collection, Fakenham, Norfolk
